敦煌壁画线描精品集

The Boutique Collection of Line Drawing of Dunhuang Mural

谢成水 绘

江苏凤凰美术出版社

图书在版编目（CIP）数据

敦煌壁画线描精品集/谢成水绘. —南京：江苏凤凰美术出版社，
2009.9（2023.8重印）
ISBN 978-7-5344-2806-7

Ⅰ.敦… Ⅱ.谢… Ⅲ.敦煌石窟—壁画—白描—作品集—中国 Ⅳ.K879.414 J222.7

中国版本图书馆CIP数据核字（2009）第084561号

选题策划	毛晓剑
责任编辑	毛晓剑
	郭 渊
装帧设计	王 主
英文翻译	施 铮
责任校对	吕猛进
责任监印	生 嫄
图片摄影	韩 祥
资料整理	谢莫兮
	华文艳
	谢玉养

责任设计编辑　龚　婷

书　　名	敦煌壁画线描精品集
绘　　者	谢成水
出版发行	江苏凤凰美术出版社（南京市湖南路1号　邮编：210009）
制　　版	南京新华丰制版有限公司
印　　刷	合肥精艺印刷有限公司
开　　本	889mm×1194mm　1/8
印　　张	16.75
版　　次	2009年9月第1版　2023年8月第12次印刷
标准书号	ISBN 978-7-5344-2806-7
定　　价	148.00元

营销部电话　025-68155675　营销部地址　南京市湖南路1号
江苏凤凰美术出版社图书凡印装错误可向承印厂调换

序

中国美术学院艺术人文学院　毛建波

得悉江苏美术出版社即将整理出版谢成水先生的敦煌壁画精品线描集，不胜欣喜。的确，原谢成水的《敦煌壁画线描集》于1998年第一次出版以来，颇受海内外艺术界的关注和喜爱。这对研究和学习中国传统绘画艺术的各大美术学院的莘莘学子而言，更是有着重要的意义。

对于研习美术者来说，敦煌无疑是心中的一座圣殿。百年前被重新发现的敦煌莫高窟，对现代美术的发展有极其巨大的影响。私认为去敦煌莫高窟朝拜、研习，或许应该是每位美术专业大学生必修的课程。我认识谢成水先生是在上世纪八十年代末的一次敦煌学国际学术研讨会上，短短几天的交往切磋，我们一见如故。之后我又二度游学敦煌，同样得到谢成水先生的盛情款待与援手相助。谢成水先生的帮助不仅仅是让我们在参观洞窟时有了更多的便利，更是以他渊博的专业知识，切中要害使我们茅塞顿开。近年来，谢成水先生又应我供职的中国美术学院聘请，为我院壁画、艺术鉴藏等专业学生授课，使我们交往更加密切，谈文论艺，受益匪浅。

谢成水先生是一位对中国古代敦煌壁画艺术研究极其认真执着的学者和艺术家。他早年曾经热衷于油画、漆画等创作，曾经在浙江美术学院（现中国美术学院）修习油画艺术。1984年，应敦煌研究院之聘，他只身一人来到敦煌莫高窟从事敦煌艺术的研究。当时他持"拿来主义"的态度，欲计划在敦煌呆上三五年，学习到一些对油画创作有益的东西便打道回府。没想到敦煌传统壁画艺术的博大精深远远超出他的想象，深深牵引挽留住他，生活在南方的他，却在敦煌一住就是二十九年。他对敦煌艺术研究的极大热情和不倦追求从未减弱，他不仅深入认真地考察了敦煌地区各处的石窟艺术，还周游各地，认真研究了麦积山、云冈、龙门、大足、新疆各地区的石窟艺术以及永乐宫壁画等。二十余年来，研究成果斐然，发表专业论文二十多篇，出版专著多部，多次在国际学术会议上宣表学术论文，赢得了国内外敦煌学家的赞誉。2002年，受英国伦敦大学邀请，谢成水先生来到大英博物馆，对收藏在那里的出自敦煌藏经洞的全部绢画进行专题研究，整整历时一年，方告完成。由于这一工作的完成，使他成为当今国内研究敦煌壁画和敦煌绢画艺术最为权威者。由于他的临摹和研究水平的高度，大英博物馆还特许他临摹了珍藏在大英博物馆，并被视为镇馆之宝的东晋顾恺之的《女史箴图》绢画。在大英博物馆的记录中，目前国内也只有他一人有机缘临摹过《女史箴图》。

当然，谢成水先生能取得上述成就，并非出于偶然。我们从他对敦煌壁画临摹线描和整理工作中的毅力和态度便可知其一斑。

在敦煌研究院，临摹莫高窟壁画是研究与保护工作的重要内容。由于临摹敦煌壁画的工作量极大，一张画一般要一两个月至半年，甚至一年。在洞窟内的临摹工作，其辛苦程度要超出常人之想象。尽管研究人员也会借用一些幻灯放大的工具，但很多部分还是需要徒手起稿拼接，所以他们的稿子往往涂改很严重，有的还多处拼接。因此，一般画完正稿之后，线描草稿已无精力再去修改整理。从2004年敦煌研究院出版的《敦煌壁画线描百图》中可以看出，很多稿子残破却无力去重新整理，只好将就出版，令人敬佩之余又不免感到一丝缺憾。有幸的是谢成水先生则在艰辛的临摹工作之余，仍坚持将所有的线描稿重新进行校对，并重新勾描翻新。有的还重勾两遍以上。其中还值得一提的是，他还喜欢将前人画过的稿子带到洞窟中去重新反复校对，然后再重新勾画。他说："这样就可以很快读懂并发现每个朝代的艺术风格的精妙之处。因为往往很精妙之处反而容易被不经意间忽略掉。"有的因为壁画破损的原因，在临摹的短时间内无法确定的线条则在校对时根据对其时代风格的反复比较和研究给予准确的肯定。这是一项极其缓慢而枯燥的工作。他第一次出版的线描集，就是他去敦煌十年之后整理的第一批线描稿。这批线描稿1996年在中国美院陈列馆展出，引起了广大师生的极大兴趣，继而结集出版。由于这样认真的研究与临摹，他的线描集引起的强烈反响，自是意料之中。谢成水先生并没有放弃对敦煌摹本线描繁重而枯燥的整理工作，在十年后的今天，他又整理出一批新的敦煌壁画线描稿，并补充了许多不同风格的线描图例，为了让后人更准确深入地学习和研究敦煌艺术。他这种高度的民族责任心和认真研究的科学态度，值得我们学习。以我的浅见陋识，谢成水先生的敦煌壁画线描集应该是研究敦煌艺术很有价值的一部线描集，也是艺术界和美术院校教学中值得推荐的一部教科书。

是为序。

己丑立夏后十日于西子湖畔养正斋，时湖色清明小荷初现

目录

1	莫高窟 272 窟（北凉） 供养菩萨 The Mogao Grottoes, Cave 272, Attendant Bodhisattvas, the Northern Liang Dynasty	17	莫高窟 285 窟（西魏） 说法图 The Mogao Grottoes, Cave 285, Buddha Preaching the Law, the Western Wei Dynasty
2	莫高窟 257 窟（北魏） 须摩提女缘品 The Mogao Grottoes, Cave 257, the Northern Wei Dynasty	18	莫高窟 428 窟（北周） 萨埵太子本生故事之一 The Mogao Grottoes, Cave 428, Jataka of Prince Sudana (Part I), the Northern Zhou Dynasty
5	莫高窟 254 窟（北魏） 萨埵太子舍身饲虎图 The Mogao Grottoes, Cave 254, Prince Sudana Attendant the Tiger, the Northern Wei Dynasty	19	莫高窟 428 窟（北周） 萨埵太子本生故事之二 The Mogao Grottoes, Cave 428, Jataka of Prince Sudana (Part II), the Northern Zhou Dynasty
6	莫高窟 254 窟（北魏） 萨埵太子舍身饲虎图（局部） The Mogao Grottoes, Cave 254, Prince Sudana Attendant the Tiger (Partial), the Northern Wei Dynasty	20	莫高窟 428 窟（北周） 萨埵太子本生故事（局部） The Mogao Grottoes, Cave 428, Jataka of Prince Sudana (Partial), the Northern Zhou Dynasty
7	莫高窟 254 窟（北魏） 萨埵太子舍身饲虎图（局部） The Mogao Grottoes, Cave 254, Prince Sudana Attendant the Tiger (Partial), the Northern Wei Dynasty	21	莫高窟 428 窟（北周） 独角仙的故事 The Mogao Grottoes, the Unicorn Story, Cave 428, the Northern Zhou Dynasty
9	莫高窟 254 窟（北魏） 尸毗王割肉贸鸽 The Mogao Grottoes, Cave 254, King Shipi Feeds the Pigeon With His Body, the Northern Wei Dynasty	22	莫高窟 420 窟（隋） 西域商队图 The Mogao Grottoes, Cave 420, the Caravan in the Western Regions, the Sui Dynasty
10	莫高窟 257 窟（北魏） 九色鹿本生故事之一、二、三 The Mogao Grottoes, Cave 254, the Jataka of the Nine-Colored Deer (Part I, II, III), the Northern Wei Dynasty	22	莫高窟 420 窟（隋） 西域商队图（局部） The Mogao Grottoes, Cave 420, the Caravan in the Western Regions (Partial), the Sui Dynasty
11	莫高窟 249 窟（西魏） 顶北披狩猎图 The Mogao Grottoes, Cave 249, Hunting(the north part of the ceiling), the Western Wei Dynasty	23	莫高窟 296 窟（北周） 善事太子入海品 The Mogao Grottoes, Cave 296, Prince Nice in the Sea, the North Zhou Dynasty
12	莫高窟 249 窟（西魏） 天宫伎乐之一、二、三 The Mogao Grottoes, Cave 249, Musicians in Heavenly Palace Part I, II, III, the Western Wei Dynasty	24	莫高窟 296 窟（北周） 善事太子入海品（局部） The Mogao Grottoes, Cave 296, Prince Nice in the Sea (Partial), the North Zhou Dynasty
13	莫高窟 249 窟（西魏） 龛内飞天之一 The Mogao Grottoes, Cave 249, Flying Apsaras Inside Niche Part I, the Western Wei Dynasty	24	莫高窟 296 窟（北周） 善事太子入海品（局部） The Mogao Grottoes, Cave 296, Prince Nice in the Sea (Partial), the North Zhou Dynasty
14	莫高窟 249 窟（西魏） 龛内飞天之二 The Mogao Grottoes, Cave 249, Flying Apsaras Inside Niche Part II, the Western Wei Dynasty	25	莫高窟 419 窟（隋） 须达拏太子本生故事之一 The Mogao Grottoes, Cave 419, Jataka of Prince Sudana Part I, the Sui Dynasty
15	莫高窟 249 窟（西魏） 龛内供养菩萨 The Mogao Grottoes, Cave 249, Attendant Bodhisattvas Inside Niche, the Western Wei Dynasty	26	莫高窟 419 窟（隋） 须达拏太子本生故事之二 The Mogao Grottoes, Cave 419, Jataka of Prince Sudana Part II, the Sui Dynasty
16	莫高窟 303 窟（北周） 观音普门品 The Mogao Grottoes, Cave 303, The Universal Door of the Bodhisattva Who Listens to the Sounds of All the World, the Northern Zhou Dynasty	27	莫高窟 419 窟（隋） 须达拏太子本生故事之三 The Mogao Grottoes, Cave 419, Jataka of Prince Sudana Part III, the Sui Dynasty
16	莫高窟 303 窟（北周） 观音普门品（局部） The Mogao Grottoes, Cave 303, The Universal Door of the Bodhisattva Who Listens to the Sounds of All the World, (Partial), the Northern Zhou Dynasty	28	莫高窟 419 窟（隋） 须达拏太子本生故事之四 The Mogao Grottoes, Cave 419, Jataka of Prince Sudana Part IV, the Sui Dynasty
16	莫高窟 303 窟（北周） 观音普门品（局部） The Mogao Grottoes, Cave 303, The Universal Door of the Bodhisattva Who Listens to the Sounds of All the World, (Partial), the Northern Zhou Dynasty	29	莫高窟 419 窟（隋） 须达拏太子本生故事之五 The Mogao Grottoes, Cave 419, Jataka of Prince Sudana Part V, the Sui Dynasty
		30	莫高窟 419 窟（隋） 须达拏太子本生故事之六 The Mogao Grottoes, Cave 419, Jataka of Prince Sudana Part VI, the Sui Dynasty
		31	莫高窟 419 窟（隋） 须达拏太子本生故事（局部） The Mogao Grottoes, Cave 419, Jataka of Prince Sudana (Partial), the Sui Dynasty
		32	莫高窟 427 窟（隋） 飞天之一、二 The Mogao Grottoes, Cave 427, Apsaras (Part I, II), the Sui Dynasty

32	莫高窟 427 窟（隋） 飞天（局部） The Mogao Grottoes, Cave 427, Apsaras (Partial), the Sui Dynasty	48	莫高窟 220 窟（唐） 北壁舞乐图（局部） The Mogao Grottoes, Cave 220, Dancers and Musicians on the North Wall (Partial), the Dang Dynasty
33	莫高窟 427 窟（隋） 飞天（局部） The Mogao Grottoes, Cave 427, Apsaras (Partial), the Sui Dynasty	49	莫高窟 220 窟（唐） 北壁舞乐图（局部） The Mogao Grottoes, Cave 220, Dancers and Musicians on the North Wall (Partial), the Dang Dynasty
34	莫高窟 427 窟（隋） 飞天（局部） The Mogao Grottoes, Cave 427, Apsaras (Partial), the Sui Dynasty	50	莫高窟 220 窟（唐） 北壁舞乐图（局部） The Mogao Grottoes, Cave 220, Dancers and Musicians on the North Wall (Partial), the Dang Dynasty
35	莫高窟 407 窟（隋） 三兔飞天藻井图案 The Mogao Grottoes, Cave 407, Three Rabbits Fling Caisson Ceiling, the Sui Dynasty	51	莫高窟 220 窟（唐） 北壁舞乐图（局部） The Mogao Grottoes, Cave 220, Dancers and Musicians on the North Wall (Partial), the Dang Dynasty
36	莫高窟 407 窟（隋） 三兔飞天藻井图案（局部） The Mogao Grottoes, Cave 407, Three Rabbits Fling Caisson Ceiling (Partial), the Sui Dynasty	52	莫高窟 220 窟（唐） 北壁舞乐图（局部） The Mogao Grottoes, Cave 220, Dancers and Musicians on the North Wall (Partial), the Dang Dynasty
37	莫高窟 276 窟（隋） 观音菩萨 The Mogao Grottoes, Cave 276, Avalokitesvara, the Sui Dynasty	53	莫高窟 220 窟（唐） 北壁舞乐图（局部） The Mogao Grottoes, Cave 220, Dancers and Musicians on the North Wall (Partial), the Dang Dynasty
38	莫高窟 57 窟（唐） 菩萨 The Mogao Grottoes, Cave 57, Bodhisattva, the Dang Dynasty	54	莫高窟 220 窟（唐） 北壁舞乐图（局部） The Mogao Grottoes, Cave 220, Dancers and Musicians on the North Wall (Partial), the Dang Dynasty
39	莫高窟 57 窟（唐） 菩萨 The Mogao Grottoes, Cave 57, Bodhisattva, the Dang Dynasty	55	莫高窟 220 窟（唐） 北壁舞乐图（局部） The Mogao Grottoes, Cave 220, Dancers and Musicians on the North Wall (Partial), the Dang Dynasty
40	莫高窟 57 窟（唐） 观无量寿经变图 The Mogao Grottoes, Cave 57, the Illustration of Amitayurdhyana Sutra, the Dang Dynasty	56	莫高窟 220 窟（唐） 北壁舞乐图（局部） The Mogao Grottoes, Cave 220, Dancers and Musicians on the North Wall (Partial), the Dang Dynasty
41	莫高窟 57 窟（唐） 观无量寿经变图（局部） The Mogao Grottoes, Cave 57, the Illustration of Amitayurdhyana Sutra (Partial), the Dang Dynasty	57	莫高窟 220 窟（唐） 北壁舞乐图（局部） The Mogao Grottoes, Cave 220, Dancers and Musicians on the North Wall (Partial), the Dang Dynasty
42	莫高窟 57 窟（唐） 观无量寿经变图（局部） The Mogao Grottoes, Cave 57, the Illustration of Amitayurdhyana Sutra (Partial), the Dang Dynasty	58	莫高窟 220 窟（唐） 北壁舞乐图（局部） The Mogao Grottoes, Cave 220, Dancers and Musicians on the North Wall (Partial), the Dang Dynasty
43	莫高窟 220 窟（唐） 南壁阿弥陀经变图（局部） The Mogao Grottoes, Cave 220, the Illustration of Amitabha Sutra on the South Wall(Partial), the Dang Dynasty	59	莫高窟 220 窟（唐） 北壁舞乐图（局部） The Mogao Grottoes, Cave 220, Dancers and Musicians on the North Wall (Partial), the Dang Dynasty
44	莫高窟 220 窟（唐） 南壁阿弥陀经变图（局部） The Mogao Grottoes, Cave 220 the Illustration of Amitabha Sutra on the South Wall(Partial), the Dang Dynasty	60	莫高窟 220 窟（唐） 北壁舞乐图（局部） The Mogao Grottoes, Cave 220, Dancers and Musicians on the North Wall (Partial), the Dang Dynasty
45	莫高窟 220 窟（唐） 北壁药师经变图（局部） The Mogao Grottoes, Cave 220, the Illustration of the Bhaisajya-guru-vaidurya-raja-sutra on the North Wall, (Partial), the Dang Dynasty		
46	莫高窟 220 窟（唐） 北壁药师经变图（局部） The Mogao Grottoes, Cave 220, the Illustration of the Bhaisajya-guru-vaidurya-raja-sutra on the North Wall, (Partial), the Dang Dynasty		
47	莫高窟 220 窟（唐） 北壁舞乐图（局部） The Mogao Grottoes, Cave 220, Dancers and Musicians on the North Wall (Partial), the Dang Dynasty		

61	莫高窟 220 窟（唐） 北壁舞乐图（局部） The Mogao Grottoes, Cave 220, Dancers and Musicians on the North Wall (Partial), the Dang Dynasty
62	莫高窟 220 窟（唐） 菩萨 The Mogao Grottoes, Cave 220, Bodhisattva, the Dang Dynasty
63	莫高窟 320 窟（唐） 菩萨 The Mogao Grottoes, Cave 320, Bodhisattva, the Dang Dynasty
64	敦煌藏经洞绢画（唐） 菩萨（英藏） Dunhuang Grottoes Silk Painting, Bodhisattva, the Dang Dynasty, Collected by Britain
65	敦煌藏经洞绢画（唐） 菩萨（英藏） Dunhuang Grottoes Silk Painting, Bodhisattva, the Dang Dynasty, Collected by Britain
66	敦煌藏经洞绢画（唐） 菩萨（英藏） Dunhuang Grottoes Silk Painting, Bodhisattva, the Dang Dynasty, Collected by Britain
67	敦煌藏经洞绢画（唐） 天王（英藏） Dunhuang Grottoes Silk Painting, Heavenly King, the Dang Dynasty, Collected by Britain
68	莫高窟 45 窟（唐） 菩萨 The Mogao Grottoes, Cave 45, Bodhisattva, the Dang Dynasty
69	莫高窟 45 窟（唐） 都督夫人像 The Mogao Grottoes, Cave 45, Portrait of Lady Command, the Dang Dynasty
70	莫高窟 444 窟（唐） 说法图 The Mogao Grottoes, Cave 444, Buddha Preaching the Law, the Dang Dynasty
71	莫高窟 329 窟（唐） 莲花飞天藻井图案 The Mogao Grottoes, Cave 329, the Lotus Apsaras Caisson Ceiling, the Dang Dynasty
72	莫高窟 329 窟（唐） 莲花飞天藻井图案（局部） The Mogao Grottoes, Cave 329, the Lotus Apsaras Caisson Ceiling (Partial), the Dang Dynasty
73	莫高窟 329 窟（唐） 飞天之二 The Mogao Grottoes, Cave 329, Apsaras (Part II), the Dang Dynasty
73	莫高窟 329 窟（唐） 飞天之一 The Mogao Grottoes, Cave 329, Apsaras (Part I), the Dang Dynasty
74	莫高窟 321 窟（唐） 飞天 The Mogao Grottoes, Cave 321, Apsaras, the Dang Dynasty
75	莫高窟 321 窟（唐） 飞天 The Mogao Grottoes, Cave 321, Apsaras, the Dang Dynasty
76	莫高窟 320 窟（唐） 舞乐图 The Mogao Grottoes, Cave 320, Dancers and Musicians, the Dang Dynasty
78	莫高窟 31 窟（唐） 菩萨 The Mogao Grottoes, Cave 31, Bodhisattva, the Dang Dynasty
79	莫高窟 217 窟（唐） 观音菩萨 The Mogao Grottoes, Cave 217, Avalokitesvara, the Dang Dynasty
80	莫高窟 23 窟（唐） 雨中耕作图 The Mogao Grottoes, Cave 23, Ploughing in the Rain, the Dang Dynasty
81	莫高窟 431 窟（唐） 马夫与马 The Mogao Grottoes, Cave 431, the Groom and the Horse, the Dang Dynasty
82	莫高窟 112 窟（唐） 反弹琵琶舞乐图 The Mogao Grottoes, Cave 112, Playing the Lute, the Dang Dynasty
84	莫高窟 112 窟（唐） 反弹琵琶舞乐图（局部） The Mogao Grottoes, Cave 112, Playing the Lute (Partial), the Dang Dynasty
85	莫高窟 112 窟（唐） 反弹琵琶舞乐图（局部） The Mogao Grottoes, Cave 112, Playing the Lute (Partial), the Dang Dynasty
86	莫高窟 112 窟（唐） 反弹琵琶舞乐图（局部） The Mogao Grottoes, Cave 112, Playing the Lute (Partial), the Dang Dynasty
87	莫高窟 45 窟（唐） 观音普门品 The Mogao Grottoes, Cave 45, the Universal Door of the Bodhisattva Who Listens to The Sounds of All the World (Partial), the Dang Dynasty
88	莫高窟 45 窟（唐） 观音普门品（局部） The Mogao Grottoes, Cave 45, the Universal Door of the Bodhisattva Who Listens to The Sounds of All the World (Partial), the Dang Dynasty
89	莫高窟 45 窟（唐） 观音普门品（局部） The Mogao Grottoes, Cave 45, the Universal Door of the Bodhisattva Who Listens to The Sounds of All the World (Partial), the Dang Dynasty
90	榆林窟 25 窟（唐） 菩萨 The Yuling Grottoes, Cave 25, Bodhisattva, the Dang Dynasty
91	榆林窟 25 窟（唐） 地藏菩萨 The Yuling Grottoes, Cave 25, The Bodhisattva Ksitigarbha, the Dang Dynasty
92	莫高窟 61 窟（五代·宋） 五台山图（局部） The Mogao Grottoes, Cave 61, the Illustration of Mount Wutai (Partial), the Five Dynasties Period-Song
92	莫高窟 61 窟（五代·宋） 五台山图（局部） The Mogao Grottoes, Cave 61, the Illustration of Mount Wutai (Partial), the Five Dynasties Period-Song
93	榆林窟 3 窟（西夏·元） 舞伎（局部） The Yuling Grottoes, Cave 3, Maiko (Partial), the Western Xia Dynasty-Yuan
93	榆林窟 3 窟（西夏·元） 舞伎（局部） The Yuling Grottoes, Cave 3, Maiko (Partial), the Western Xia Dynasty-Yuan
93	榆林窟 3 窟（西夏·元） 舞伎 The Yuling Grottoes, Cave 3, Maiko, the Western Xia Dynasty-Yuan

| 94 | 莫高窟 409 窟（西夏） 回鹘王礼佛图
The Mogao Grottoes, Cave 409,
King Huigu Worshiping Buddha, the Western Xia Dynasty |
| --- | --- |
| 95 | 莫高窟 328 窟（西夏） 菩萨
The Mogao Grottoes, Cave 328,
Bodhisattva, the Western Xia Dynasty |
| 96 | 榆林窟 3 窟（西夏·元） 文殊菩萨
The Yuling Grottoes, Cave 3,
Wenshu Buddha, the Western Xia Dynasty–Yuan |
| 97 | 榆林窟 3 窟（西夏·元） 文殊菩萨（局部）
The Yuling Grottoes, Cave 3,
Wenshu Buddha (Partial), the Western Xia Dynasty-Yuan |
| 98 | 榆林窟 3 窟（西夏·元） 文殊菩萨（局部）
The Yuling Grottoes, Cave 3,
Wenshu Buddha (Partial), the Western Xia Dynasty-Yuan |
| 99 | 榆林窟 3 窟（西夏·元） 普贤菩萨
The Yuling Grottoes, Cave 3,
Puxian Buddha, the Western Xia Dynasty-Yuan |
| 100 | 榆林窟 3 窟（西夏·元） 普贤菩萨（局部）
The Yuling Grottoes, Cave 3,
Puxian Buddha (Partial), the Western Xia Dynasty-Yuan |
| 101 | 榆林窟 3 窟（西夏·元） 普贤菩萨（局部）
The Yuling Grottoes, Cave 3,
Puxian Buddha (Partial), the Western Xia Dynasty-Yuan |
| 102 | 莫高窟 465 窟（元） 菩萨
The Mogao Grottoes, Cave 465,
Bodhisattva, the Yuan Dynasty |
| 103 | 莫高窟 320 窟（元） 菩萨
The Mogao Grottoes, Cave 320,
Bodhisattva, the Yuan Dynasty |
| 104 | 莫高窟 61 窟（元） 供养比丘
The Mogao Grottoes, Cave 61,
Attendant the Monk, the Yuan Dynasty |
| 105 | 莫高窟 61 窟（元） 供养比丘尼
The Mogao Grottoes, Cave 61,
Attendant the Bhiksuni, the Yuan Dynasty |
| 106 | 莫高窟 3 窟（元） 千手千眼观音菩萨
The Mogao Grottoes, Cave 3,
Thousand-armed and Thousand-eyed Avalokitesvara, the Yuan Dynasty |
| 107 | 莫高窟 3 窟（元） 千手千眼观音菩萨（局部）
The Mogao Grottoes, Cave 3,
Thousand-armed and Thousand-eyed Avalokitesvara (Partial), the Yuan Dynasty |
| 108 | 莫高窟 3 窟（元） 千手千眼观音菩萨（局部）
The Mogao Grottoes, Cave 3,
Thousand-armed and Thousand-eyed Avalokitesvara (Partial), the Yuan Dynasty |
| 109 | 莫高窟 3 窟（元） 千手千眼观音菩萨（局部）
The Mogao Grottoes, Cave 3,
Thousand-armed and Thousand-eyed Avalokitesvara (Partial), the Yuan Dynasty |
| 110 | 莫高窟 3 窟（元） 千手千眼观音菩萨（局部）
The Mogao Grottoes, Cave 3,
Thousand-armed and Thousand-eyed Avalokitesvara (Partial), the Yuan Dynasty |
| 111 | 莫高窟 3 窟（元） 千手千眼观音菩萨（局部）
The Mogao Grottoes, Cave 3,
Thousand-armed and Thousand-eyed Avalokitesvara (Partial), the Yuan Dynasty |
| 112 | 莫高窟 3 窟（元） 千手千眼观音菩萨（局部）
The Mogao Grottoes, Cave 3,
Thousand-armed and Thousand-eyed Avalokitesvara (Partial), the Yuan Dynasty |
| 113 | 莫高窟 3 窟（元） 千手千眼观音菩萨（局部）
The Mogao Grottoes, Cave 3,
Thousand-armed and Thousand-eyed Avalokitesvara (Partial), the Yuan Dynasty |
| 114 | 莫高窟 3 窟（元） 千手千眼观音菩萨（局部）
The Mogao Grottoes, Cave 3,
Thousand-armed and Thousand-eyed Avalokitesvara (Partial), the Yuan Dynasty |
| 115 | 莫高窟 3 窟（元） 千手千眼观音菩萨（局部）
The Mogao Grottoes, Cave 3,
Thousand-armed and Thousand-eyed Avalokitesvara (Partial), the Yuan Dynasty |
| 116 | 莫高窟 3 窟（元） 千手千眼观音菩萨（局部）
The Mogao Grottoes, Cave 3,
Thousand-armed and Thousand-eyed Avalokitesvara (Partial), the Yuan Dynasty |
| 117 | 顾恺之女史箴图（东晋） 仕女（局部）（英藏）
Lady Officials by Gu Kaizhi,
Ladies(Partial), Collected by Britain |
| 117 | 附　录
Appendix |
| 118 | 东晋　顾恺之《女史箴图》（局部）
Lady Officials by Gu Kaizhi (Partial),
the Eastern Jin Dynasty |
| 119 | 新疆克孜尔 80 窟　听法图
Kezier, Xinjiang, Cave 80,
Listening the Law |
| 120 | 西藏萨迦南寺壁画　欢喜金刚
Mural in Sakya South Temple, Tibet,
Happy Vajra |
| 121 | 山西永乐宫壁画（元） 玉女
Mural in Yongle Palace, Shanxi,
Teenage Girl |
| 122 | 山西永乐宫壁画（元） 白虎君
Mural in Yongle Palace, Shanxi,
White Tigar |
| 123 | 印度雕刻（公元 1-3 世纪） 少女
Indian Carving (1st-3rd century)Girl |
| 124 | 后记
Postscript |

莫高窟 272 窟（北凉） 供养菩萨
The Mogao Grottoes, Cave 272 , Attendant Bodhisattvas, the Northern Liang Dynasty

莫高窟 257 窟（北魏） 须摩提女缘品
The Mogao Grottoes, Cave 257, the Northern Wei Dynasty

莫高窟 254 窟（北魏） 萨埵太子舍身饲虎图
The Mogao Grottoes, Cave 254, Prince Sudana Attendant the Tiger, the Northern Wei Dynasty

莫高窟 254 窟（北魏） 萨埵太子舍身饲虎图（局部）
The Mogao Grottoes, Cave 254, Prince Sudana Atterdant the Tiger (Partial), the Northern Wei Dynasty

莫高窟 254 窟（北魏） 萨埵太子舍身饲虎图（局部）
The Mogao Grottoes, Cave 254, Prince Sudana Attendant the Tiger (Partial), the Northern Wei Dynasty

莫高窟 254 窟（北魏） 尸毗王割肉贸鸽
The Mogao Grottoes, Cave 254, King Shipi Feeds the Pigeon With His Body, the Northern Wei Dynasty

莫高窟 257 窟（北魏） 九色鹿本生故事之一、二、三
The Mogao Grottoes, Cave 254, the Jataka of the Nine-Colored Deer (Part I, II, III), the Northern Wei Dynasty

莫高窟 249 窟（西魏） 顶北披狩猎图
The Mogao Grottoes, Cave 249, Hunting (the north part of the ceiling), the Western Wei Dynasty

莫高窟 249 窟（西魏） 天宫伎乐之一、二、三
The Mogao Grottoes, Cave 249, Musicians in Heavenly Palace Part I, II, III, the Western Wei Dynasty

莫高窟 249 窟（西魏） 龛内飞天之一
The Mogao Grottoes, Cave 249, Flying Apsaras Inside Niche Part I, the Western Wei Dynasty

莫高窟 249 窟（西魏） 龛内飞天之二
The Mogao Grottoes, Cave 249, Flying Apsaras Inside Niche Part II, the Western Wei Dynasty

莫高窟 249 窟（西魏） 龛内供养菩萨
The Mogao Grottoes, Cave 249, Attendant Bodhisattvas Inside Niche, the Western Wei Dynasty

莫高窟 303 窟（北周）　观音普门品
The Mogao Grottoes, Cave 303, The Universal Door of the Bodhisattva Who Listens to the Sounds of All the World, the Northern Zhou Dynasty

莫高窟 303 窟（北周）　观音普门品（局部）
The Mogao Grottoes, The Universal Door of the Bodhisattva Who Listens to the Sounds of All the World, (Partial), Cave 303, the Northern Zhou Dynasty

莫高窟 303 窟（北周）　观音普门品（局部）
The Mogao Grottoes, Cave 303, The Universal Door of the Bodhisattva Who Listens to the Sounds of All the World, (Partial), the Northern Zhou Dynasty

莫高窟 285 窟（西魏） 说法图
The Mogao Grottoes, Cave 285, Buddha Preaching the Law, the Western Wei Dynasty

莫高窟 428 窟（北周） 萨埵太子本生故事之一
The Mogao Grottoes, Cave 428, Jataka of Prince Sudana (Part I), the Northern Zhou Dynasty

莫高窟 428 窟（北周） 萨埵太子本生故事之二
The Mogao Grottoes, Cave 428, Jataka of Prince Sudana (Part II), the Northern Zhou Dynasty

莫高窟 428 窟（北周） 萨埵太子本生故事（局部）
The Mogao Grottoes, Cave 428, Jataka of Prince Sudana (Partial)the Northern Zhou Dynasty

莫高窟 428 窟（北周） 独角仙的故事
The Mogao Grottoes, Cave 428, the Unicorn Story, the Northern Zhou Dynasty

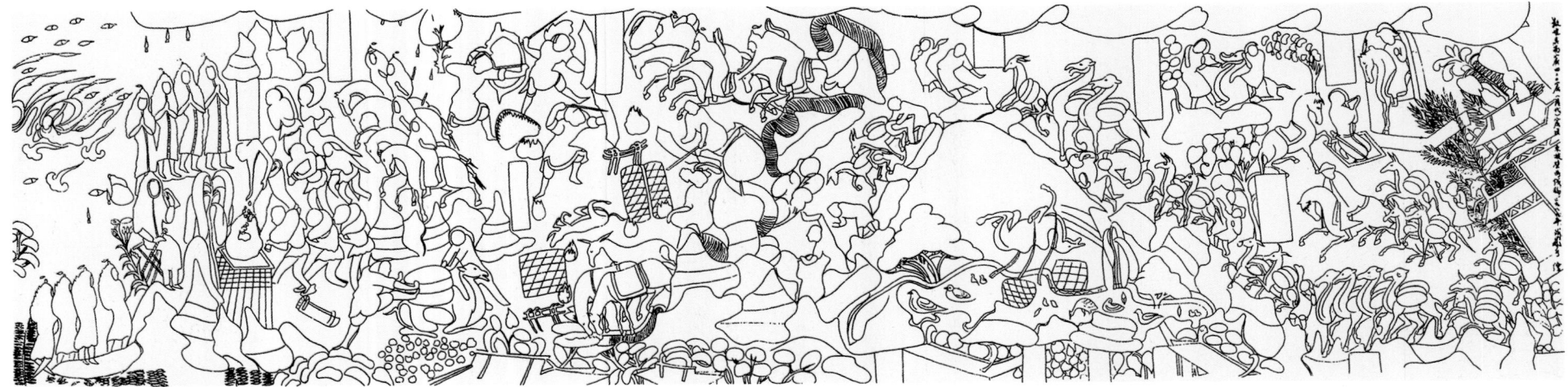

莫高窟 420 窟（隋） 西域商队图
The Mogao Grottoes, Cave 420, the Caravan in the Western Regions, the Sui Dynasty

莫高窟 420 窟（隋） 西域商队图（局部）
The Mogao Grottoes, Cave 420, the Caravan in the Western Regions (Partial), the Sui Dynasty

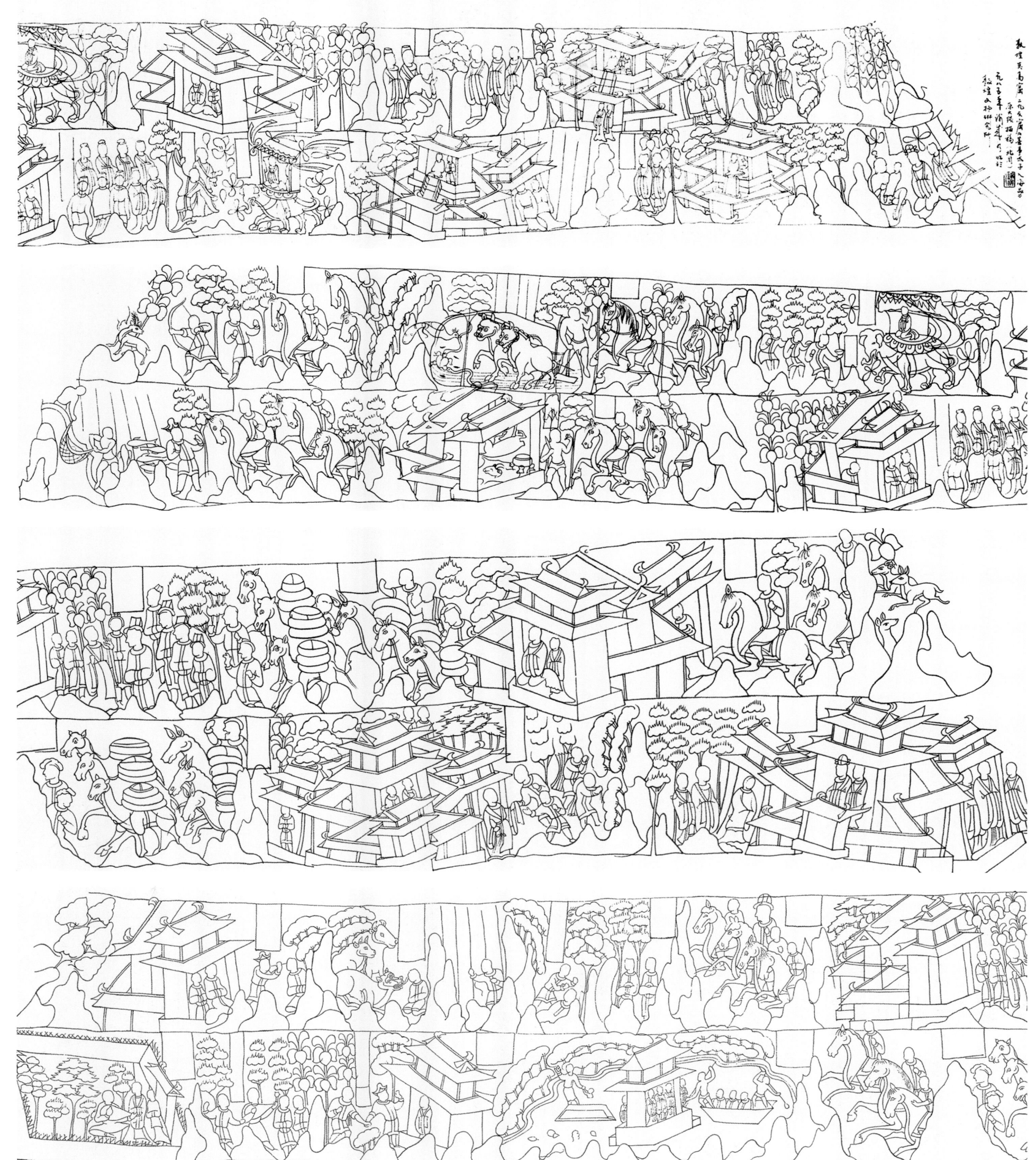

莫高窟 296 窟（北周） 善事太子入海品
The Mogao Grottoes, Cave 296, Prince Nice in the Sea, the North Zhou Dynasty

莫高窟 296 窟（北周） 善事太子入海品（局部）
The Mogao Grottoes, Cave 296, Prince Nice in the Sea (Partial), the North Zhou Dynasty

莫高窟 296 窟（北周） 善事太子入海品（局部）
The Mogao Grottoes, Cave 296, Prince Nice in the Sea (Partial), the North Zhou Dynasty

莫高窟 419 窟（隋） 须达拏太子本生故事之一
The Mogao Grottoes, Cave 419, Jataka of Prince Sudana Part I, the Sui Dynasty

莫高窟 419 窟（隋） 须达拏太子本生故事之二
The Mogao Grottoes, Cave 419, Jataka of Prince Sudana Part II, the Sui Dynasty

莫高窟 419 窟（隋） 须达拏太子本生故事之三
The Mogao Grottoes, Cave 419, Jataka of Prince Sudana Part III, the Sui Dynasty

莫高窟 419 窟（隋） 须达拏太子本生故事之四
The Mogao Grottoes, Cave 419, Jataka of Prince Sudana Part IV, the Sui Dynasty

莫高窟 419 窟（隋） 须达拏太子本生故事之五
The Mogao Grottoes, Cave 419, Jataka of Prince Sudana Part V, the Sui Dynasty

莫高窟419窟（隋） 须达拏太子本生故事之六
The Mogao Grottoes, Cave 419, Jataka of Prince Sudana Part VI, the Sui Dynasty

莫高窟 419 窟（隋） 须达拏太子本生故事（局部）
The Mogao Grottoes, Cave 419, Jataka of Prince Sudana (Partial), the Sui Dynasty

莫高窟 427 窟（隋） 飞天之一、二
The Mogao Grottoes, Cave 427, Apsaras (Part I, II), the Sui Dynasty

莫高窟 427 窟（隋） 飞天（局部）
The Mogao Grottoes, Cave 427, Apsaras (Partial), the Sui Dynasty

莫高窟 427 窟（隋） 飞天（局部）
The Mogao Grottoes, Cave 427, Apsaras (Partial), the Sui Dynasty

莫高窟 427 窟（隋） 飞天（局部）
The Mogao Grottoes, Cave 427, Apsaras (Partial), the Sui Dynasty

莫高窟 407 窟（隋） 三兔飞天藻井图案
The Mogao Grottoes, Cave 407, Three Rabbits Fling Caisson Ceiling, the Sui Dynasty

莫高窟 407 窟（隋） 三兔飞天藻井图案（局部）
The Mogao Grottoes, Cave 407, Three Rabbits Fling Caisson Ceiling (Partial), the Sui Dynasty

莫高窟 276 窟（隋） 观音菩萨
The Mogao Grottoes, Cave 276, Avalokitesvara, the Sui Dynasty

莫高窟 57 窟（唐） 菩萨
The Mogao Grottoes, Cave 57, Bodhisattva, the Dang Dynasty

莫高窟 57 窟（唐） 菩萨
The Mogao Grottoes, Cave 57, Bodhisattva, the Dang Dynasty

莫高窟 57 窟（唐） 观无量寿经变图
The Mogao Grottoes, Cave 57, the Illustration of Amitayurdhyana Sutra, the Dang Dynasty

莫高窟 57 窟（唐） 观无量寿经变图（局部）
The Mogao Grottoes, Cave 57, the Illustration of Amitayurdhyana Sutra (Partial), the Dang Dynasty

莫高窟 57 窟（唐） 观无量寿经变图（局部）
The Mogao Grottoes, Cave 57, the Illustration of Amitayurdhyana Sutra (Partial), the Dang Dynasty

莫高窟 220 窟（唐） 南壁阿弥陀经变图（局部）
The Mogao Grottoes, Cave 220, the Illustration of Amitabha Sutra on the South Wall(Partial), the Dang Dynasty

莫高窟 220 窟（唐） 南壁阿弥陀经变图（局部）
The Mogao Grottoes, Cave 220, the Illustration of Amitabha Sutra on the South Wall(Partial), the Dang Dynasty

莫高窟 220 窟（唐） 北壁药师经变图（局部）
The Mogao Grottoes, Cave 220, the Illustration of the Bhaisajya-guru-vaidurya-raja-sutra on the North Wall, (Partial), the Dang Dynasty

莫高窟 220 窟（唐） 北壁药师经变图（局部）
The Mogao Grottoes, Cave 220, the Illustration of the Bhaisajya-guru-vaidurya-raja-sutra on the North Wall, (Partial), the Dang Dynasty

莫高窟 220 窟（唐） 北壁舞乐图（局部）
The Mogao Grottoes, Cave 220, Dancers and Musicians on the North Wall (Partial), the Dang Dynasty

莫高窟 220 窟（唐） 北壁舞乐图（局部）
The Mogao Grottoes, Cave 220, Dancers and Musicians on the North Wall (Partial), the Dang Dynasty

莫高窟 220 窟（唐）北壁舞乐图（局部）
The Mogao Grottoes, Cave 220, Dancers and Musicians on the North Wall (Partial), the Dang Dynasty

莫高窟 220 窟（唐） 北壁舞乐图（局部）
The Mogao Grottoes, Cave 220, Dancers and Musicians on the North Wall (Partial), the Dang Dynasty

莫高窟 220 窟（唐） 北壁舞乐图（局部）
The Mogao Grottoes, Cave 220, Dancers and Musicians on the North Wall (Partial), the Dang Dynasty

莫高窟 220 窟（唐） 北壁舞乐图（局部）
The Mogao Grottoes, Cave 220, Dancers and Musicians on the North Wall (Partial), the Dang Dynasty

莫高窟 220 窟（唐） 北壁舞乐图（局部）
The Mogao Grottoes, Cave 220, Dancers and Musicians on the North Wall (Partial), the Dang Dynasty

莫高窟 220 窟（唐） 北壁舞乐图（局部）
The Mogao Grottoes, Cave 220, Dancers and Musicians on the North Wall (Partial), the Dang Dynasty

莫高窟 220 窟（唐） 北壁舞乐图（局部）
The Mogao Grottoes, Cave 220, Dancers and Musicians on the North Wall (Partial), the Dang Dynasty

莫高窟 220 窟（唐） 北壁舞乐图（局部）
The Mogao Grottoes, Cave 220, Dancers and Musicians on the North Wall (Partial), the Dang Dynasty

莫高窟 220 窟（唐） 北壁舞乐图（局部）
The Mogao Grottoes, Cave 220, Dancers and Musicians on the North Wall (Partial), the Dang Dynasty

莫高窟 220 窟（唐） 北壁舞乐图（局部）
The Mogao Grottoes, Cave 220, Dancers and Musicians on the North Wall (Partial), the Dang Dynasty

莫高窟 220 窟（唐） 北壁舞乐图（局部）
The Mogao Grottoes, Cave 220, Dancers and Musicians on the North Wall (Partial), the Dang Dynasty

莫高窟 220 窟（唐） 北壁舞乐图（局部）
The Mogao Grottoes, Cave 220, Dancers and Musicians on the North Wall (Partial), the Dang Dynasty

莫高窟 220 窟（唐） 北壁舞乐图（局部）
The Mogao Grottoes, Cave 220, Dancers and Musicians on the North Wall (Partial), the Dang Dynasty

莫高窟 220 窟（唐） 菩萨
The Mogao Grottoes, Cave 220, Bodhisattva, the Dang Dynasty

莫高窟 320 窟（唐） 菩萨
The Mogao Grottoes, Cave 320, Bodhisattva, the Dang Dynasty

敦煌藏经洞绢画（唐） 菩萨（英藏）
Dunhuang Grottoes Silk Painting, Bodhisattva, the Dang Dynasty, Collected by Britain

敦煌藏经洞绢画（唐） 菩萨（英藏）
Dunhuang Grottoes Silk Painting, Bodhisattva, the Dang Dynasty, Collected by Britain

敦煌藏经洞绢画（唐） 菩萨（英藏）
Dunhuang Grottoes Silk Painting, Bodhisattva, the Dang Dynasty, Collected by Britain

敦煌藏经洞绢画（唐） 天王（英藏）
Dunhuang Grottoes Silk Painting, Heavenly King, the Dang Dynasty, Collected by Britain

莫高窟 45 窟（唐） 菩萨
The Mogao Grottoes, Cave 45, Bodhisattva, the Dang Dynasty

莫高窟 45 窟（唐） 都督夫人像
The Mogao Grottoes, Cave 45, Portrait of Lady Command, the Dang Dynasty

莫高窟 444 窟（唐） 说法图
The Mogao Grottoes, Cave 444, Buddha Preaching the Law, the Dang Dynasty

莫高窟 329 窟（唐） 莲花飞天藻井图案
The Mogao Grottoes, Cave 329, the Lotus Apsaras Caisson Ceiling, the Dang Dynasty

莫高窟 329 窟（唐） 莲花飞天藻井图案（局部）
The Mogao Grottoes, Cave 329, the Lotus Apsaras Caisson Ceiling (Partial), the Dang Dynasty

莫高窟 329 窟（唐） 飞天之一
The Mogao Grottoes, Cave 329, Apsaras (Part I), the Dang Dynasty

莫高窟 329 窟（唐） 飞天之二
The Mogao Grottoes, Cave 329, Apsaras (Part II), the Dang Dynasty

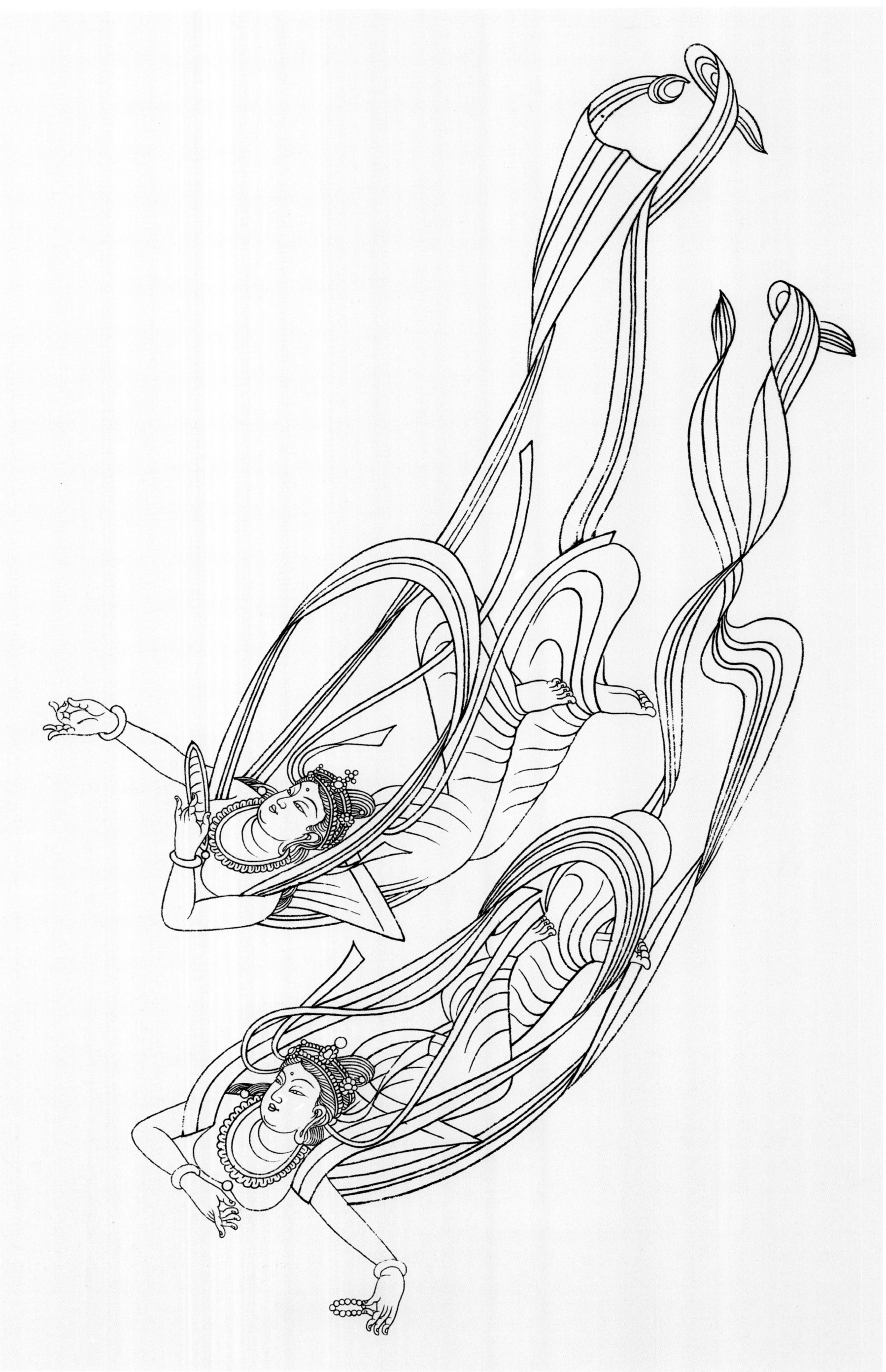

莫高窟 321 窟（唐） 飞天
The Mogao Grottoes, Cave 321, Apsaras, the Dang Dynasty

莫高窟 321 窟（唐） 飞天
The Mogao Grottoes, Cave 321, Apsaras, the Dang Dynasty

莫高窟 320 窟（唐） 舞乐图
The Mogao Grottoes, Cave 320, Dancers and Musicians, the Dang Dynasty

莫高窟 31 窟（唐） 菩萨
The Mogao Grottoes, Cave 31, Bodhisattva, the Dang Dynasty

莫高窟 217 窟（唐） 观音菩萨
The Mogao Grottoes, Cave 217, Avalokitesvara, the Dang Dynasty

莫高窟 23 窟（唐） 雨中耕作图
The Mogao Grottoes, Cave 23, Ploughing in the Rain, the Dang Dynasty

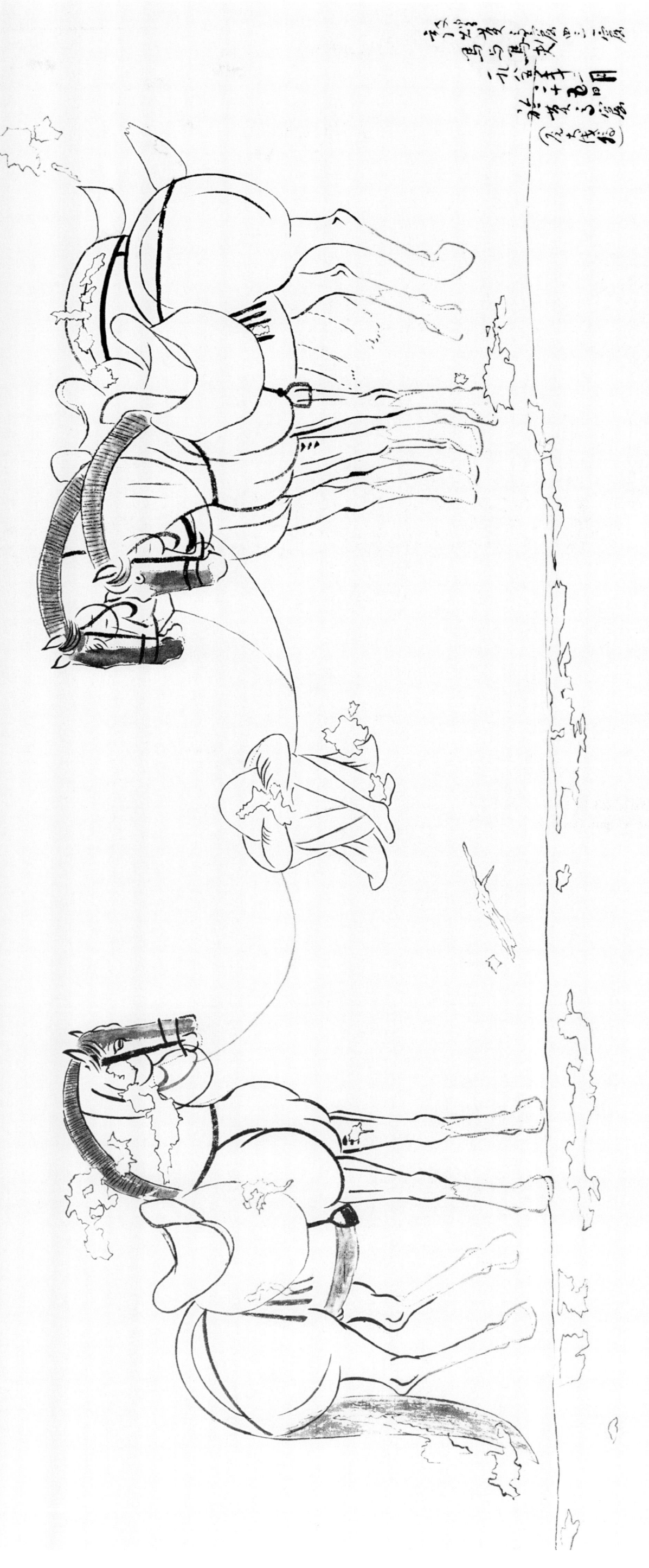

莫高窟 431 窟（唐） 马夫与马
The Mogao Grottoes, Cave 431, the Groom and the Horse, the Dang Dynasty

莫高窟 112 窟（唐） 反弹琵琶舞乐图
The Mogao Grottoes, Cave 112, Playing the Lute, the Dang Dynasty

莫高窟 112 窟（唐） 反弹琵琶舞乐图（局部）
The Mogao Grottoes, Cave 112, Playing the Lute (Partial), the Dang Dynasty

莫高窟 112 窟（唐） 反弹琵琶舞乐图（局部）
The Mogao Grottoes, Cave 112, Playing the Lute (Partial), the Dang Dynasty

莫高窟 112 窟（唐） 反弹琵琶舞乐图（局部）
The Mogao Grottoes, Cave 112, Playing the Lute (Partial), the Dang Dynasty

莫高窟 45 窟（唐） 观音普门品
The Mogao Grottoes, Cave 45, the Universal Door of the Bodhisattva Who Listens to The Sounds of All the World (Partial), the Dang Dynasty

莫高窟 45 窟（唐） 观音普门品（局部）
The Mogao Grottoes, Cave 45, the Universal Door of the Bodhisattva Who Listens to The Sounds of All the World (Partial), the Dang Dynasty

莫高窟 45 窟（唐） 观音普门品（局部）
The Mogao Grottoes, Cave 45, the Universal Door of the Bodhisattva Who Listens to The Sounds of All the World (Partial), the Dang Dynasty

榆林窟 25 窟（唐） 菩萨
The Yuling Grottoes, Cave 25, Bodhisattva, the Dang Dynasty

地藏菩薩

榆林窟 25 窟（唐） 地藏菩萨
The Yuling Grottoes, Cave 25, The Bodhisattva Ksitigarbha, the Dang Dynasty

莫高窟 61 窟（五代・宋） 五台山图（局部）
The Mogao Grottoes, Cave 61, the Illustration of Mount Wutai (Partial), the Five Dynasties Period-Song

莫高窟 61 窟（五代・宋） 五台山图（局部）
The Mogao Grottoes, Cave 61, the Illustration of Mount Wutai (Partial), the Five Dynasties Period-Song

榆林窟 3 窟（西夏·元） 舞伎
The Yuling Grottoes, Cave 3, Maiko, the Western Xia Dynasty-Yuan

榆林窟 3 窟（西夏·元） 舞伎（局部）
The Yuling Grottoes, Cave 3, Maiko (Partial), the Western Xia Dynasty-Yuan

榆林窟 3 窟（西夏·元） 舞伎（局部）
The Yuling Grottoes, Cave 3, Maiko (Partial), the Western Xia Dynasty-Yuan

莫高窟 409 窟（西夏） 回鹘王礼佛图
The Mogao Grottoes, Cave 409, King Huigu Worshiping Buddha, the Western Xia Dynasty

莫高窟 328 窟（西夏） 菩萨
The Mogao Grottoes, Cave 328, Bodhisattva, the Western Xia Dynasty

榆林窟 3 窟（西夏·元） 文殊菩萨
The Yuling Grottoes, Cave 3, Wenshu Buddha, the Western Xia Dynasty-Yuan

榆林窟 3 窟（西夏·元） 文殊菩萨（局部）
The Yuling Grottoes, Cave 3, Wenshu Buddha (Partial), the Western Xia Dynasty-Yuan

榆林窟 3 窟（西夏·元） 文殊菩萨（局部）
The Yuling Grottoes, Cave 3, Wenshu Buddha (Partial), the Western Xia Dynasty-Yuan

榆林窟 3 窟（西夏·元） 普贤菩萨
The Yuling Grottoes, Cave 3, Puxian Buddha, the Western Xia Dynasty-Yuan

榆林窟3窟（西夏·元） 普贤菩萨（局部）
The Yuling Grottoes, Cave 3, Puxian Buddha (Partial), the Western Xia Dynasty-Yuan

莫高窟 465 窟（元） 菩萨
The Mogao Grottoes, Cave 465, Bodhisattva, the Yuan Dynasty

莫高窟 320 窟（元） 菩萨
The Mogao Grottoes, Cave 320, Bodhisattva, the Yuan Dynasty

莫高窟 61 窟（元） 供养比丘
The Mogao Grottoes, Cave 61, Attendant the Monk, the Yuan Dynasty

莫高窟 61 窟（元） 供养比丘尼
The Mogao Grottoes, Cave 61, Attendant the Bhiksuni, the Yuan Dynasty

莫高窟 3 窟（元） 千手千眼观音菩萨
The Mogao Grottoes, Cave 3, Thousand-armed and Thousand-eyed Avalokitesvara, the Yuan Dynasty

莫高窟 3 窟（元） 千手千眼观音菩萨（局部）
The Mogao Grottoes, Cave 3, Thousand-armed and Thousand-eyed Avalokitesvara (Partial), the Yuan Dynasty

莫高窟 3 窟（元） 千手千眼观音菩萨（局部）
The Mogao Grottoes, Cave 3, Thousand-armed and Thousand-eyed Avalokitesvara (Partial), the Yuan Dynasty

莫高窟 3 窟（元） 千手千眼观音菩萨（局部）
The Mogao Grottoes, Cave 3, Thousand-armed and Thousand-eyed Avalokitesvara (Partial), the Yuan Dynasty

莫高窟 3 窟（元） 千手千眼观音菩萨（局部）
The Mogao Grottoes, Cave 3, Thousand-armed and Thousand-eyed Avalokitesvara (Partial), the Yuan Dynasty

莫高窟 3 窟（元） 千手千眼观音菩萨（局部）
The Mogao Grottoes, Cave 3, Thousand-armed and Thousand-eyed Avalokitesvara (Partial), the Yuan Dynasty

莫高窟 3 窟（元） 千手千眼观音菩萨（局部）
The Mogao Grottoes, Cave 3, Thousand-armed and Thousand-eyed Avalokitesvara (Partial), the Yuan Dynasty

莫高窟 3 窟（元） 千手千眼观音菩萨（局部）
The Mogao Grottoes, Cave 3, Thousand-armed and Thousand-eyed Avalokitesvara (Partial), the Yuan Dynasty

莫高窟 3 窟（元） 千手千眼观音菩萨（局部）
The Mogao Grottoes, Cave 3, Thousand-armed and Thousand-eyed Avalokitesvara (Partial), the Yuan Dynasty

莫高窟 3 窟（元） 千手千眼观音菩萨（局部）
The Mogao Grottoes, Cave 3, Thousand-armed and Thousand-eyed Avalokitesvara (Partial), the Yuan Dynasty

莫高窟 3 窟（元） 千手千眼观音菩萨（局部）
The Mogao Grottoes, Cave 3, Thousand-armed and Thousand-eyed Avalokitesvara (Partial), the Yuan Dynasty

附录

顾恺之女史箴图（东晋） 仕女（局部）（英藏）
Lady Officials by Gu Kaizhi, Ladies(Partial), Collected by Britain

东晋　顾恺之《女史箴图》（局部）
Lady Officials by Gu Kaizhi (Partial), the Eastern Jin Dynasty

新疆克孜尔80窟 听法图
Kezier, Xinjiang, Cave 80, Listening the Law

西藏萨迦南寺壁画　欢喜金刚
Mural in Sakya South Temple, Tibet, Happy Vajra

山西永乐宫壁画（元） 玉女
Mural in Yongle Palace, Shanxi, Teenage Girl

山西永乐宫壁画（元） 白虎君
Mural in Yongle Palace, Shanxi, White Tigar

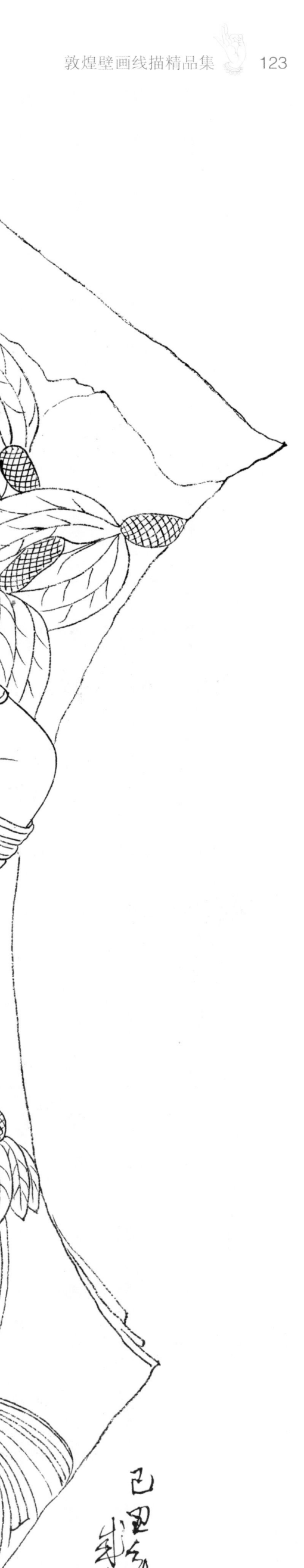

印度雕刻（公元1-3世纪）　少女
Indian Carving (1st-3rd century) Girl

后记

1982年我正在当时的浙江美术学院（现为中国美术学院）油画系进修油画，一次偶然的机会，在一本杂志上看到外国的一位艺术批评家写道：到目前为止，中国没有一个人深入研究了西方艺术，也没有一个人深入研究了自己的东方艺术。我很震惊，虽然我们所处的时候不容去学习古代，但是不可能连一个人也没有过深入研究？于是我利用暑假的二个月自费从杭州出发前往龙门、永乐宫、西安、麦积山、云岗、大足、敦煌考察中国古代艺术。当我最后到敦煌时，我又一次震惊，这里竟然留存了中国十个朝代近一千多年的艺术真迹，而我们仅知其皮毛。这是一座世界绝无仅有的艺术宝库！西方现代艺术家们从远古的东方艺术寻找养料充实了他们。我非常理解常书鸿先生为什么一个人从法国回来能坚持在敦煌研究几十年。当然，还有一批随常书鸿先生在一起默默研究了几十年的同志，但力量毕竟太小。所以，日本人夸口说："敦煌在中国，研究在日本。"敦煌回来后，心情久久无法平静，于是向中央写了一封建议信，建议在敦煌设立一所"敦煌艺术进修学院"，希望能为国内外艺术家在这里研究学习提供方便。我决定去敦煌工作，正好当时敦煌研

作者在永福寺大佛泥塑制作现场

作者在莫高窟工作照

作者在大英博物馆临摹《女史箴图》

究院向全国招聘研究人员，我报了名，当时全国有34名画画的人报了名，我想这下人多力量大了。但结果只去成了我一个人。听说有一个应聘的画家早上到了莫高窟，下午就跑走了。我是南方福建人，因为当时条件的确较差，特别莫高窟的水是苦泉水，喝了会拉肚子，我只好买了一只塑料大桶，每个星期从城里背两次淡水食用。一直背了三年，后来莫高窟改善生活，有专用大汽车拉水了，才停止自己背水。我是1984年10月到莫高窟的，到了莫高窟后才知道，我写到中央的建议信，被转到邓小平办公室，再又转至文化部，当时的文化部长朱穆之批复给国家文物局，文物局又转批到了敦煌研究院，同意安排筹建，可是国家不给钱。1986年上半年，院长要我出去化缘，我走了大半个中国，那个年代化缘不是那么容易，另外还有种种原因，所以至今未能建成。那年化缘回来后我便潜心研究敦煌艺术。让我重视敦煌壁画线稿的事是1986年研究院安排我临摹北魏254窟《舍身饲虎》图时，发现稿子和壁画有的地方不对，254窟《舍身饲虎》图是北魏时期的杰作，早在抗日战争时期，由董希文先生临过，现存的线稿是他当时直接在墙上拷贝下来的。理当是准确无误的。但我到洞窟上色时才发现，仍有许多细节不对。特别是画面中心的山脚没有画出来，这样就使整个画面的环境不明确，如悬在山坡上，这幅画的整个环境是在一个群山环抱中的一块平地间发生的事。后来我又查阅了董希文先生当时的临本，他果然没有在意。另外还有部分细节被忽略掉了。对于这样一幅伟大的杰作，不应该有这样的失误。因为在这之前，我在中国美

院曾看过老师临摹这幅壁画，也是用这张原大稿子画的，以为原本就是这样的。我感到这个事情重大，一张稿子一传十，十传百，贻误后人就严重了。自此之后我便对每张稿子都要到洞窟的原画前进行校对，尽量地争取更准确，有的反复校对好几次，因为有的看不清，有的是由多个人起过的稿子，各有不同。这样的工作，对我研究敦煌艺术起到了很大的帮助，使我很快深入地了解到各时代的笔法线法，同时也发现了敦煌十个朝代各种风格的精妙之处，并且寻找到了中国绘画各个时期的演变过程。当然，在莫高窟主要的工作任务是进洞窟临摹壁画，稍微了解敦煌壁画临摹的人都知道，这是一项非常艰苦的工作。我们要求临本都必须是原大尺寸，敦煌壁画人物众多，场景繁杂，要凭空起稿临摹是很困难的事。当年张大千先生去敦煌时，也感到起稿的困难，于是他用毛边纸直接从墙上拷贝下来。尽管如此，这位临摹高手还是没有把握直接在壁上勾好线条，只好想了一个窍门，用毛笔在要勾的线上点上无数个虚点点，然后放在平面上再重新勾勒成线稿，最后拷贝到正稿上去。当然，这种方法现在是绝对禁止的。我们唯一能借助的就是幻灯机，将拍好的底片由幻灯机放大到稿纸上，然后在纸上用铅笔做出大概的位置和各种记号。为什么说是"大概"位置呢？也许只有用过幻灯机放稿的人才知道，幻灯机放出的线条走近看时都是模糊不定的。幻灯机上的底片烤热了随时都在变长变宽。另外，任何照相机拍出的底片都有不同程度的四周透视变形。如果是大幅画必须用十几张底片，放大时，每张底片的四边都无法与原作合拢。所以每张底片有用率只能到百分之六七十左右，其余四边都得靠凭空起稿。我第一次临摹不知其中原故，修完稿后才与原作尺寸对比，竟每边各长出75公分，使我两个月的时间前功尽弃。幻灯机放完稿后，必须进洞慢慢地一点一点校对修正成肯定的线条。这一段时间特别长，几乎占全画完成的一半以上时间。我

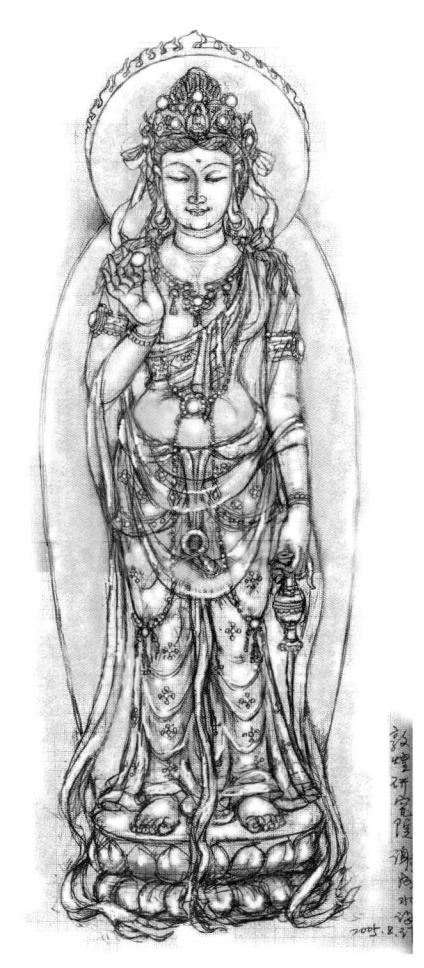

杭州韬光寺宝珠观音塑像
（6米脱胎漆）草图谢成水设计

宝珠观音泥塑完成稿

们每临摹一张画都得几个月或半年，甚至更长的时间。按我们标准的工作量，每月修稿量约为两平方米左右。所以，我们的稿子基本上是认真的。当然修完后的线稿也是很难看的，上面不仅很脏，还有不少挖补的"补丁"，因为变形部分必须挖成喇叭形才能接上，涂改的线条只有自己认得。最后拷贝到正稿上去。待正稿完成后，这张稿子也折腾得差不多了，所以必须再整理。但画完之后想要将这些稿子再去重新整理勾描一遍，恐怕每个人都有一种不堪回首的后怕。由于以上种种原因，我们每个人的稿子准确度都会因人而异。有的会留下部分线条待在正稿上再画。特别是早期的壁画，我们只在线稿上画出第一遍土红色的起稿线，第二遍的墨线在正稿完成时才能勾上。如这里的249、285、303、428等窟的线稿就是这样的。有时我们同事之间也会互相交换一些自己喜欢的线稿，但经过上次的教训后，我都得亲自一一校对过，有时甚至校对两遍以上。当然我也不可能做到完全绝对的准确，还望有心者继续校正和完善。我之所以有机会再次整理重新描绘旧稿，并装裱成轴，还得感谢原中国美院肖锋院长的邀请，要我在美院作一次敦煌壁画线描展。才迫使我花了一年多的时间，整理去敦煌十多年的线描稿，并于1996年在中国美术学院陈列馆展出，受到前辈和老师同学们的欢迎和喜爱。1998年又由甘肃人民美术出版社第一次汇编成《谢成水敦煌壁画线描集》出版。这已是十年前的事了。

2002年，我受到英国伦敦大学的邀请和赞助，去英国研究大英博物馆内收藏的敦煌藏经洞绢画。这对我来说是一生中最大的愿望。因为敦煌艺术中包括壁画、彩塑和藏经洞绢画三大部分，唯独绢画全部流失在国外。而绢画中的线法笔法及其绘画技法，正与历代卷轴画相同，特别是卷轴画兴盛的今天，其研究意义更为重要。我在英国整理研究了

一年，才完成全部四百多个编号的敦煌绢画（包括未公布的）这项巨大的研究工程。这里面还得感谢英国伦敦大学的韦陀教授（Roderick Whitfield）和夫人朴英淑教授的大力帮助，让我免费吃住在他家中一年，才使我顺利完成了系统研究敦煌绢画的工作。在这期间还受到爱国华人林玮女士和其丈夫邓家祥先生的大力赞助。在大英博物馆斯坦因密室阅览敦煌绢画期间，同时也看到了同在密室中的东晋顾恺之的《女史箴图》，这幅被誉为中国最早的绢画也是大英博物馆的镇馆之宝。也许因为我的临摹技巧和在国际学术界的影响，才被特许在密室里临摹了《女史箴图》，这使我此次的绢画研究获得了意料之外的巨大收获，使我真正体悟到了古代绘画所谓的"高古游丝描"。

杭州永福寺大雄宝殿一佛二弟子（9米）
雕塑设计草图 谢成水设计

永福寺大佛铸铜完成照

在研究中国绘画的各种线描技法同时，也逐渐开始研究中国古代雕塑中的塑造。因为在中国古代，画与雕塑都是相通的。在敦煌的艺术中，很多洞窟的画塑都是同一个人完成，其最重要的一点就是造型线法相通。2003年，我为英国东方艺术研究机构绘制向联合国申请修复阿富汗五世纪的巴米扬50米大佛的复原图和效果图（见英国东方艺术杂志）。2006年正式为杭州灵隐寺旁的永福大寺塑造唐代风格的9米高的青铜大佛和弟子像，接着为杭州韬光寺制作唐代风格的宝珠观音，均受到了各界的好评。2006年我任南京师范大学敦煌学研究中心副主任、教授。2007年应邀为北京奥运会"鸟巢"体育馆内总统休息厅设计了56扇传统技法的雕漆屏风。2009年被中国美术学院公共艺术学院聘为客座教授、硕士生导师。

由于自己研究或教学的需要，我每年都要抽时间继续整理敦煌壁画线描稿。听日本留学回来的朋友讲，在日本的东京艺术大学和其它艺术院校里都有把我的线描集作为教材来教授敦煌艺术课程，这使我更感到责任的重大以及重要意义。十年又过去了，感谢江苏美术出版社再次将我的敦煌线描稿重新汇编成集，不仅加入了近十年的作品，而且做了精选。在此也向诸位师长及同仁作一个汇报。这里汇集了中国十个朝代历时一千余年的具有代表性的敦煌壁画线描稿，并且清晰地呈现出这些线条的演变过程。例如北凉、北魏的线条明显受西域和印度的影响，线条精细偏向装饰性，但线条的画法仍赋予了中国绘画和书法的情感，特别是在底层的起稿线上完全可以看到汉代画像砖的传统笔法；西魏时期受南方东晋顾恺之"秀骨清像"造型影响，线条纤细，用笔飘逸；北周开始转向中国传统的大篆笔法，中锋圆浑有力；隋代造型以秀美灵动居多，线条挺直而长，如急风直过，但另一派也用粗犷的中锋笔法出现，为唐代奠定了基础；唐代造型线条壮美而富丽，完成了汉民族书法绘画线条的完美表现时期，用笔粗壮肥实有力，以中锋笔法为主，线条工整，变化讲究，飘带线条多作"当风"之卷动。当然，笔法的风格在唐代各时期也各有不同；宋代以后，则线条多变，出现了皴擦的笔法；元代时期，由于中原宋代兴起的水墨画此时才反馈到敦煌之故，线条的风格变得丰富多样，除了继承了唐宋的线条用笔之外，还有文人水墨画的笔法和染法，也有如宋徽宗的"瘦金体"笔法，同时也出现了来自印度影响的藏传佛教密宗的装饰线条画法。当然，元代又大大地突破了唐代的线条表现，不仅线条壮实有力，且粗细并用，转折依形而走，变化多端，使线条表现的生动性和情感推向了一个极高的峰巅。对于怎样学习和研究传统艺术的问题上，我认为临摹是重要的。而在"临"与"摹"的二者之间，我更主张多"临"，"临"会使人更快"读"懂画的原意。哪怕是认真地临一只手，一个头或是一块很小的画面，都会很快地有所收获。因为"临"更能发现细微变化，而一个伟大杰作的精妙处往往就在这细微之中。这也可以算是我的一点心得吧。